A PARADE FOR
George Washington

by DAVID A. ADLER

illustrated by JOHN O'BRIEN

HOLIDAY HOUSE • NEW YORK

George Washington was the commander in chief of the Continental Army during the American Revolution. He led the fight to free the thirteen American colonies from the mighty king of England. With their victory, the colonies became the United States of America.

After the war Washington went home to Virginia. He was there when the new United States Congress chose our first president. Every vote was for Washington.

On Tuesday, April 14, 1789, the secretary of the Congress arrived at Washington's home with the news. Washington would take an oath and assume his new position in New York City, the capital of the new nation. He would go there by horse and carriage. The trip would take one week.

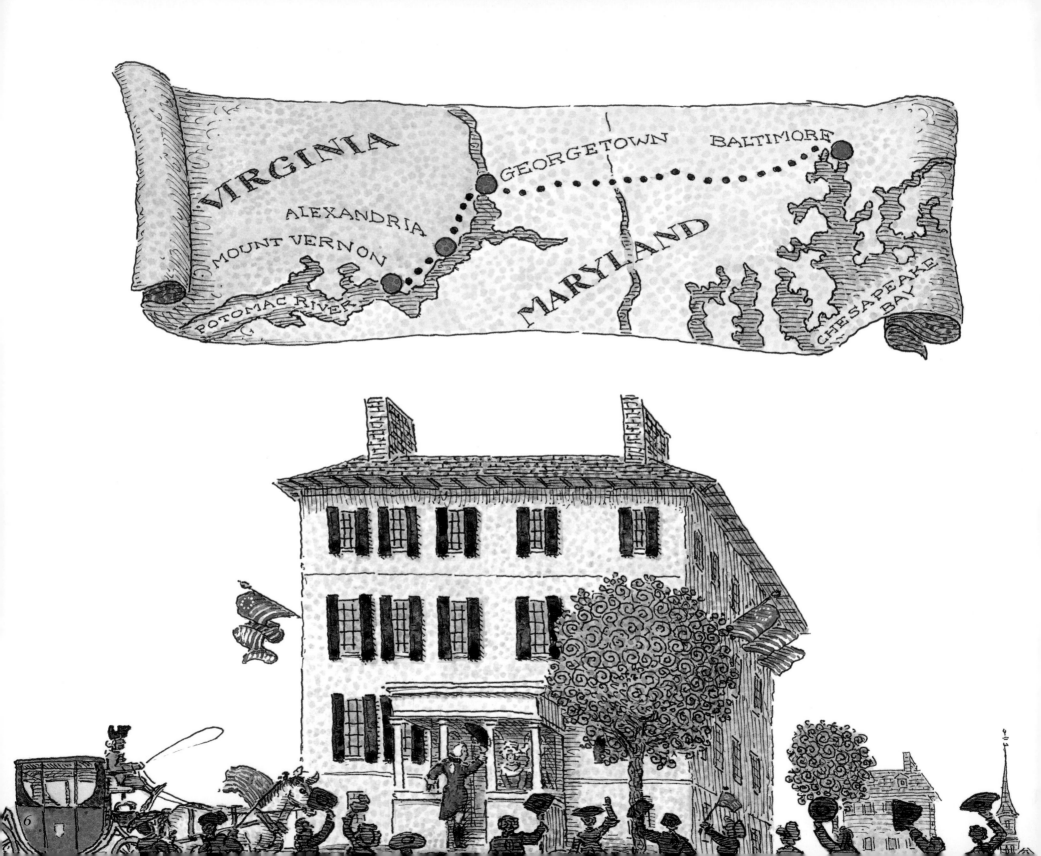

George Washington's first stop was nearby Alexandria, Virginia, where his neighbors gave a dinner in his honor. "Words fail me," Washington said that night. "I bid all my affectionate friends and kind neighbors farewell."

The next morning George Washington rode north.
People came from every farmhouse and shop to greet him.
All along the way they stood by the sides of the road and
cheered. In each village he passed, they rang bells and fired
rifles to honor him.

A crowd met him outside Baltimore and rode with him
into the city. At night there was a party for George Washington.
In the morning a cannon was fired in his honor. Then there was
a parade as the leading citizens of Baltimore rode north with him
for seven miles.

9

George Washington rode on through Delaware.

He crossed into Pennsylvania, where the governor and a troop of soldiers met him. They rode together to Chester. There he mounted a beautiful white horse and rode in a makeshift parade into Philadelphia.

People lined the streets of the city. Washington waved, and they waved back, calling out at every step, "Long live George Washington!"

That night at a party, people cheered for Washington. The next day there was to be a parade of soldiers for him, but it was raining.

Washington told the soldiers to stay inside. He wanted them to keep out of the rain.

He continued through Pennsylvania and into New Jersey. George Washington waved as he rode into Trenton, and people cheered. They had built a huge arch of branches, leaves, and flowers. As Washington passed beneath the arch, young girls all dressed in white robes, each with a crown of leaves on her head, threw flowers in his path and sang a song written for the occasion by future New Jersey governor Richard Howell.

The many others who came out to greet him called out, "Long live Washington!"

Teary-eyed George Washington took off his hat, waved it, and rode on.

Throughout New Jersey there were parties and parades.
All the hoopla was a bit much for George Washington.
He wanted to enter New York City quietly, but the people of
New York wouldn't let him.

At Elizabeth Town, New Jersey, he left his carriage and stepped
onto a large flatboat prepared for his arrival in New York City.
It had thirteen oarsmen, one for each state in the new nation.
Each wore a white shirt and black cap.

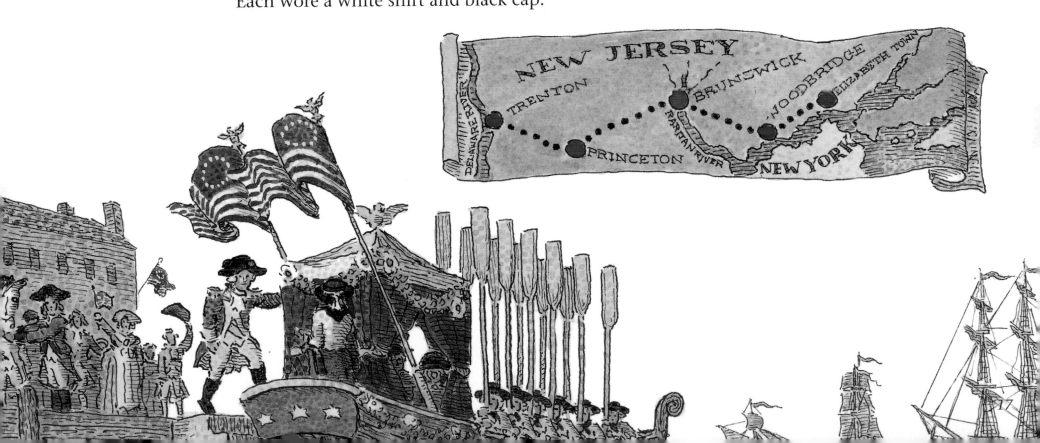

When Washington stepped onto the boat, people
along the shore sent up a long and deafening shout.
At a signal, each oarsman put his oar in the water and
trumpets sounded, followed by loud marching music.

Other boats decked with banners, flags, and streamers joined Washington's. It was a parade on water, a parade of boats.

19

As Washington approached the harbor he passed two anchored boats. On board were parties of men and women who sang songs composed just for him.

Another ship, the *Galveston*, was quiet until Washington came close. Then suddenly it came alive with banners, flags, and a thirteen-gun salute.

"The display of boats," Washington wrote in his diary, "the decorations of the ships, the roar of cannon . . . filled my mind with sensations."

At the dock a military escort stood ready to protect Washington, but he dismissed them. "I require no guard," he said.

The governor of the state, the mayor of the city, religious leaders, foreign ministers, and regular citizens accompanied him to the house in which he would stay, yet another parade for George Washington.

One week later, church bells rang in New York City. There was a parade of carriages. George Washington, dressed in a dark-brown suit, his hair tied back and powdered, rode in the last carriage. Many people walked behind his carriage.

The parade stopped at Federal Hall. Soldiers lined both sides of
the street, and Washington walked between them and into the hall.

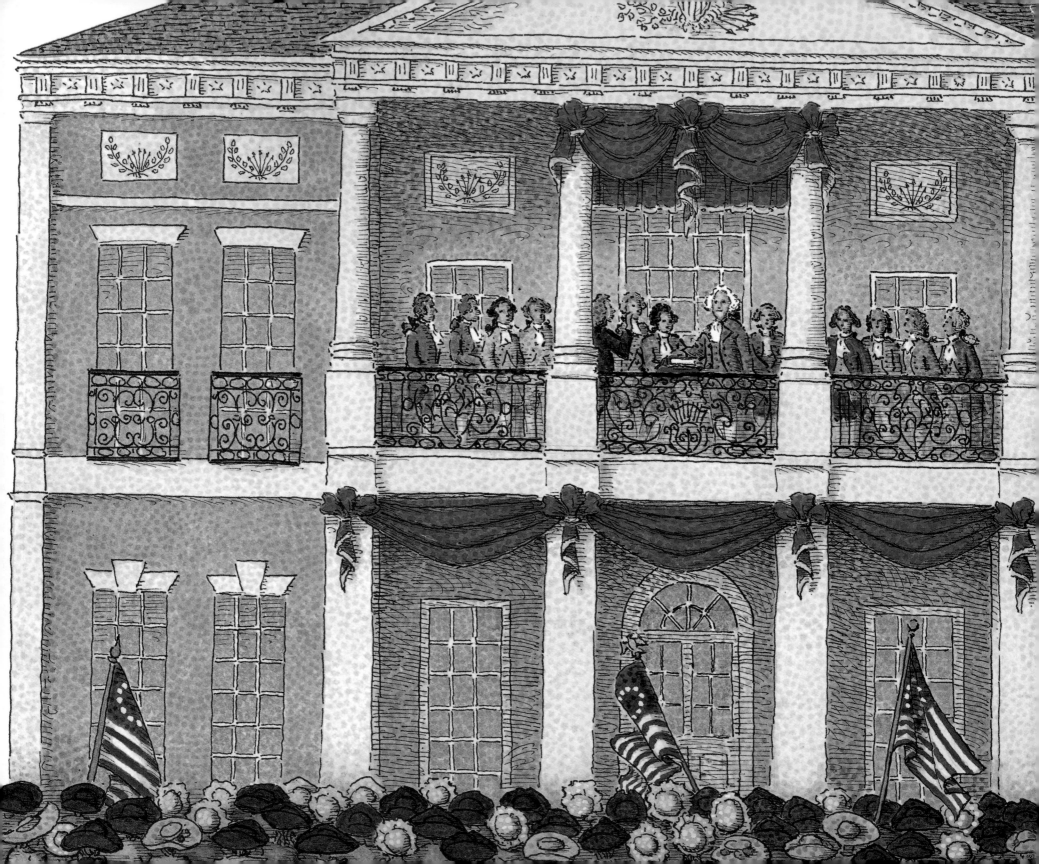

He stood on the upper porch, and thousands of people cheered from their windows, rooftops, and the street below. He placed his hand on his heart and bowed a few times to the people outside.

Samuel Otis, secretary of the Senate, held a red velvet pillow. On it was an open Bible. Washington put his hand on the Bible. New York State chancellor Robert R. Livingston read the oath of office and Washington repeated it. He promised to "preserve, protect, and defend the Constitution of the United States." Washington then kissed the Bible and added to the oath, "So help me God."

27

The people outside cheered. They were sure George Washington would be a great first president.
And he was.

Important Dates in George Washington's Life

1732   Born in Virginia, February 22.

1752   Appointed an officer in the Virginia militia.

1759   Married Martha Dandridge Custis, January 6.

1775   First battles of the American Revolutionary War at Lexington and Concord, Massachusetts, April 19.

1776   The Declaration of Independence approved by Congress, July 4.

1783   Treaty of Paris is signed, ending the Revolution, September 3.

1789   Took oath as the first president of the United States, April 30.

1792   Reelected president, December 5.

1799   Died at his Mount Vernon home, December 14.

SOURCE NOTES

p. 7   "Words fail me . . . kind neighbors farewell." Lodge, p. 43.

p. 14   "Strew your hero's way with flowers," that the young girls of Trenton sang; "Long live George Washington," that others called out; and the description of Washington sailing into New York harbor are from Headley, p. 434.

p. 14   That the song was written by Governor Howell is from Whipple, p. 210.

p. 16   That Washington preferred to quietly enter New York Harbor is from Irving, p. 253, and Whipple, p. 210.

p. 21   The description of the two boats crowded with revelers in New York Harbor is from Irving, p. 253.

p. 21   "The display of boats . . . filled my mind with sensations," Marshall, p. 267. The sensations, Washington wrote, were both "pleasing" as they reflected so many people's trust in him and "painful (contemplating the reverse of this scene which may be the case after all my labors to do good)."

p. 22   "I require no guard," is from Paulding, p. 168.

p. 22   The reception Washington received from New York officials, religious leaders, foreign ministers, and regular citizens is from Headley, p. 408.

p. 27   That Washington kissed the Bible and added "So help me God" is from Kirkland, p. 438.

BIBLIOGRAPHY

Headley, Joel T. *The Illustrated Life of Washington*. New York: G. & F. Bill, 1860.

Irving, Washington. *The Life of Washington*, volume 2. New York: G. P. Putnam and Co., 1859.

Kirkland, Caroline M. *Memoirs of Washington*. London: D. Appleton & Co., 1857.

Lodge, Henry Cabot. *George Washington*, volume 2. Boston: Houghton Mifflin, 1889.

Marshall, John. *The Life of George Washington*. Philadelphia: Lea and Blanchard and P. H. Nicklin, 1838.

Paulding, James K. *A Life of Washington*, volume 2. New York: Harper & Brothers, 1840.

Sparks, Jared. *Life of George Washington*. Boston: Ferdinand Andrews, 1839.

Whipple, Wayne. *The Story-Life of Washington: A Life-History in Five Hundred True Stories*, Philadelphia: John C. Winston Co., 1911.

Let's make a parade for
Kate and John Briggs
—D. A. A.

For Linda
—J. O.

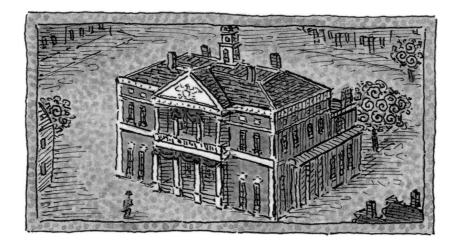

Text copyright © 2020 by David A. Adler
Illustrations copyright © 2020 by John O'Brien
All Rights Reserved
HOLIDAY HOUSE is registered in the U.S. Patent and Trademark Office.
Printed and bound in April 2023 at Leo Paper, Heshan, China.
The art was created with Rapidograph pens and Dr. Ph. Martin's Hydrus Fine Art Watercolors
on Strathmore 500 series Vellum Bristol paper.
www.holidayhouse.com
First hardcover edition, 2020
First paperback edition, 2023
3 5 7 9 10 8 6 4 2

Library of Congress Cataloging-in-Publication Data

Names: Adler, David A., author. | O'Brien, John, 1953–illustrator.
Title: A parade for George Washington / by David A. Adler ; illustrated by John O'Brien.
Description: First edition. | New York : Holiday House, [2020] | Includes
bibliographical references. | Audience: Ages 7–10 | Audience: Grades 4–6
Summary: "Follows George Washington's journey from Virginia to New
York in anticipation of his inauguration at Federal Hall in New York
City on April 30, 1789"—Provided by publisher.
Identifiers: LCCN 2019022763 | ISBN 9780823442522 (hardcover)
Subjects: LCSH: Washington, George, 1732-1799—Inauguration, 1789—Juvenile
literature. | Presidents—United States—Inauguration—Juvenile literature.
Classification: LCC E312.66 .A355 2020 | DDC 973.4/1092—dc23
LC record available at https://lccn.loc.gov/2019022763

ISBN: 978-0-8234-4252-2 (hardcover)
ISBN: 978-0-8234-5468-6 (paperback)